The Wind and Its Waves

WRITTEN BY LISA OSORIO
ILLUSTRATED BY MELISSA HOLTZER

Ibukku is an auto-publishing company. The content of this work is the responsibility of the author and do not necessarily reflect the views of the publisher.

The Wind and its Waves
Written by Lisa Osorio
Illustrated by Melissa Holtzer
Published by Ibukku.
www.Ibukku.com
Graphic design: Índigo Estudio Gráfico
Copyright © 2018 Lisa Osorio
ISBN Paperback: 978-1-64086-229-6
ISBN eBook: 978-1-64086-230-2
Library of Congress Control Number: 2018953393

Acknowledgments:

First and foremost, I have to thank Alek Juarez and Ibukku for making this dream of mine a reality.

To my parents, thank you for always encouraging me and supporting me when I become doubtful. For being a constant light and encourager and most importantly, for always believing in me.

To Daisy, thank you for offering your assistance and guidance in every new venture I chose to partake in. You never hesitate to offer a helping hand. Thank you.

To my soul sisters, Vicky, India, May: Thank you for filling a valuable place in my life and heart. Your support and love has me overwhelmed with joy.

To my family, thank you for pushing me to be better, do better and to explore my creativity.

Melissa, thank you for collaborating with me through your artwork. You are an incredible artist and am eternally grateful for you.

Lastly, to my supporters and friends,

Thank you for your love, support, and kindness. I do this for me, but also for you. Writing is a part of my peace and I hope that this book releases love, connectedness, calmness, and clarity.

I love you all,

Lisa Osorio

Illustrated by Melissa Holtzer

"I use words to touch your heart and art to inspire your mind".

Email: meliccious@gmail.com

IG: b.stung

Welcome
04/24/17

These inked stained hands will not stop writing
I write to heal, to breakthrough, to recover
To effectively practice my therapy
I hope that you receive value from this cleansing that I do
That you get every drop of insight life has thrown at me
As if everything I go through is to better create you
May we grow together
Enjoy

A New Season 2018
02/28/18

In every new season, there is an open door to step up,
with new problems arising, new values, and a new sense of
self and awareness.
My character building, respect blossoming so beautifully
and love appearing in places that have needed attention and
healing.
There is still an old me attempting to stick to antiquated
habits,
but a renewed mind is present.
My vision is more powerful than my challenges.
I am not alone.

Authentic Speaker
12/21/16

there's gentleness in your voice,
when you speak amongst the crowd
they become present by your words
they listen
so that they can hear their hearts speak.
you direct them to their inner child
a part of them that's not as present.
you redirect
you bring them focus
you dial their specific code
that gets them to reach
the rawest human energy

Tell Me
11/28/16

Tell me, Tell me
Did you love me?
Because you ripped pieces from me
Now all I have are bits and pieces of me

Prison Gates
11/11/16

Your love dissipates
Then like the words I speak to you; it disintegrates
Right outside your mental prison gates
Will you ever learn to love without your boring ordinariness?
Or will you have her make you feel your emptiness
Wish your parents loved you at an earlier age
So your expressions of love don't have to be muted and caged
See my love was trained, practiced, and was offered to you;
intact
With much purity, sensibility, stability
All the qualities that you lack
And you had no will to change
After I had poured my life, my spirit, my strengths
But isn't that strange
What you said coming from your lips was never congruent
with how we spent our days
Can you believe we saw a future--- of us getting engaged?
Yet, you were more motivated in maintaining to be the same
You couldn't do it, you couldn't change
I sit still not feeling enraged
I left you
I'm unbroken, untamed
You left me here shocked, amazed
Unbothered, unafraid
This is the decision I've made

11

Everlasting Soul
12/21/16

Speak
Speak to me
You're enjoying the avoidance
You keep neglecting me
Seeking comfort that's resulting in ignorance
If you listen softly,
You can feel
Everything
All the things I've placed in you
To execute

Before you leave this world,
I'll help you gather your thoughts
I'll guide you to unfold
To understand how beautiful
Your wounds are in this earth
You will bloom

I am your everlasting soul
That is seeking your undivided attention.
It's time that you listen
To the calling of you

Silent Misery
12/31/16

Sparkles arise
The sun hides as the moon peeks through the clouds
She is viewing life differently
With flashes of her spiritual awakening
She can hear the birds chirping
She sails around her own imagination
Exploring the depths of her
She's a wild girl seeking adventure
She is free to be
She is letting herself escape
Her silent misery.

All Nighters
1/07/17

How can I resist this
He listens
He's patient
As I spoke with words for soul revelations
Till the rise of dawn.
He's kind
He hugs
Me in his warmth
As my tears soaked his arms.

Attention Ladies
1/09/17

Fall in love with the beauties on this earth
But careful princess
Don't let the world fall so deep into you.
This is your Queendom.
Don't let the kingdom own you.

Drunk Note to Self
1/14/17

The way you treat me in public
tells me
everything
I need to know
towards how I should treat you
in private.

Soul Mirrors
12/31/16

Once we break silence,
I get to know myself more
You're so intellectual.
You find my thoughts
That were wandering inside
My mind divides and multiplies
You bring the rush of life
And I can feel my insides burning
Tears in my eyes
The madness in this world
Triggers us to uplift humanity
Your soul mirrors mine.

Pretty
01/11/17

Next time you call me pretty, finish your sentence.
Pretty witty. Pretty intelligent. Pretty genuine.
I am beyond beauty
I crave a compliment that is worth remembering.
Not open to surface level compliments
That fall into the category of objectifying women.
Describe my spirit, compliment me from the inside.
Remind me that my physique won't define me.
Tell me,
I'm beyond pretty.

A Beauty in the Flesh
01/23/17

She listens more than she speaks.
She learns techniques
To strengthen weak, elevate our central beliefs
Motivate, appreciate,
Donate knowledge, educate humanity
She's willing to grow, to read more
All for a higher force.
She's coated with thick skin.
Drenched with love; compassion.
Rooted with sensitivity & an ability to encourage.
She's moved mountains with her mind.
She maintains her optimism.
When life gives her mazes
That are not in her best interest
And she is led to misfortune,
She opens up the doors to her
Tenderness, affection, kindness.
She receives the revelation.
She sacrifices her ego and her pride,
To pursue a calling greater than her.
Contributing to the greater good.
Her composure; polished..
We applaud her for it.
The people refer to her as,
you.

Broken Girl
01/25/17

Darling,
Why do you have the need to see others turn cold?
You have contempt towards other women.
You share the same body parts with them.
You are dissing on your own female presence.
You are speaking words of abuse to other reflections of you.
I don't want to begin
To imagine
Your wounds, I'm sensing your energy. Antipathetic.
Your overconfidence is a platform of insecurity
Instilled in you that feeds your ego.
You carry heavy baggage
And your lack of understanding
Is causing you unprecedented tantrums.
Your dark minds filled with hatred, unforgiveness.
You are stirring the recipe to wicked, poison.
Darling,
When will you be open enough
To confess your brokenness and seek forgiveness?
Till then,
Your bitterness will conquer your clouded, misguided
perceptions.

A Humbling Thought
07/18/17

Comparing either
assassinates confidence
Or
Enhances the ego
Look within and reflect

We are all leaves of different colors
Coming from the same tree
Brothers and sisters and friends with
Different wavelengths
How can you say the moon is better
Than the stars
Or the sun
Or the galaxies?

Loss of Love Reflections
1/30/17

echoes of solitude
her face expressions.

she is alone
the only thing following her,
shadows.

abandoned.

healed by self
now poured through her veins
an abundance of self-compassion
saved by pain

Her isolation
made her great.
indestructible.

1/30/17

Your love is a past due homework assignment
You put in work when it's too late
You take advantage of my time
And bribe me to give you another chance.
But sweetheart,
If you can't respect my time,
Why shall I respect yours?
You'll turn it in once I get sick of waiting.
Surprise, surprise
I won't accept it.

-homework DENIED

September Lessons
01/31/17

Silence your voice when he reaches out to you through his
friends.
Tell them, you are just fine.
Hush their mouths when they ask you about him and if you
miss him.
Just smile. Distract them.
When that day comes and he bumps into you,
You will notice his nervousness.
Let him feel his emotions,
Let him vent and when he asks you how you are doing,
lie.
Don't you dare plant a seed of doubt in his mind
That you aren't happy without him.
Don't feed into his energy.
Lie if you have to
So you can remind yourself of the bigger picture.
You deserve a king

Cold hearted
05/15/17

You're going to miss me when I'm gone
I won't be crying any longer
The tears I shed aren't sufficient
They aren't flowing like rivers, they're small puddles
I've recovered.
My rainforest has transformed to drought.
Pat on the back for me,
For I have survived you.

Odd Impact
05/15/17

Intelligent
Your brain is lightning.
It processes information in the most effective manner
Gifted
Your abilities to conversate, relate, negotiate are
well- practiced.
Perfectly sharpened.
Manipulative
The severity of your selfishness made me conform to you
Aggressive
The sharp tone in your voice,
The frustrating impulses popping out of your veins
Forming fists with your hands during our altercations.
Your personality stirred a storm in me,
Yet built firm soil.
Yes, both simultaneously
And now, I'm trying to figure it out.
How to let it all out of me

Sweet Souls
05/15/17

It's those that have built me up with words
Of encouragement that have prevented me from breaking
Those same souls have been selective
With their words when I need to wake up
No sugar coating but sensitive when it comes to my heart

MIA
04/16/18

I came from the ocean
the waves brought me ashore
lost myself in tears
found myself here

The wind and its waves
brought me
pieces of me

Pieces of peace
scattered all over
rivers and seas
the waves
caused my comfort and clarity
while the wind brought the hell out of me
and I'm grateful for the balance
because,
my growth from it all
is never- ending.

Brave Men

Bring out the men with their own opinion
Men that think for themselves
Men that open doors, impact our children,
Willing to learn the language of
Our love,
The ones that think of our needs, and
That purposefully finds ways
To crack out smiles within us
When nothing feels right.
Show us the warriors
Who influence and understand
Who have an equal balance of vulnerability and strength
Too many weak men
Hanging on to our glorious women
Help us,
Help them

Don't Bother
04/16/18

Drunk in my solitude
My defenses are high
But I am fine
Keeping myself inside
This little box of mine
Because if I don't
There's no place else
To hide
Respect
My recovery time

No Codepency
08/10/17

The pain you offer me
It's tempting
I can almost take it,
Put the blame on you
And call myself victim
But blaming you
Defeats
Me

Masochist
08/10/17

Hurt me, so I can write my heart out
And discover more of my aliveness
With your constant rejection

Good On My Own
08/17/17

Have
Control
Have
Hope
Choose
Love

That's what they tell me
I'm not fighting with that
But how about
Become the person
You are seeking for

Romance yourself
Find joy in the
Independence
Have
Self-reliance

Rather than filling up a broken, empty bottle
It's better to fix the bottle then fill it up.
Or else, it will keep leaking
And it will never always be full.

Bad Intentions
02/09/17

She is a jewel to be reckoned with
Yet you noticed her outer material
And didn't focus on the canvas of her mind
She is soft like candy that's cotton
Yet you didn't appreciate her sensitivity
And you would put in effort to see her rough
To see her destruct and give her blossom
To fuck.
She is a gift to the world
But a piece of pleasure in yours.

Independence
07/18/17

And now that you're alone
You walk a road less traveled by
Most compromise their bliss for comfort
And always wonder how it feels
To live on the edges of things
But do not execute on it
And when they are alone
They seek someone
You seek yourself
And we all admire you for this

Rotten Guests
03/28/18

sharing me is like
cutting the roots from a tree

I am here to stay
rooted to this ground

safe space
where I am honored
where I bare fruit
and joined as one
with this world of mine
I share enough resources here

I am not a home
that has
too many
guests in the evening

I am divine property
not the city museum

coming here for a ride?
loosen your seat belt
you're not safe here.
come in here
with the wrong intentions
the consequences
will be your host

humbled
02/11/17

what I've been struggling with,
you have given me strength in.

The Sweetest Revenge
02/18/17

The best revenge
Begins with learning
The techniques
To love yourself more
And with that love
You filter out the bitterness
Through the medicine of time
You seek forgiveness
You don't learn to lose love for them
You simply drench yourself with your spirit
With the intent of worthiness
And you will reject the abusive
The best revenge
Is to not seek it

Ex Best Friend
02/17/17

It's not you I miss.
It's the friendship
That melts away our defenses
Vulnerable and open conversations
That made our hearts ponder
Life's unresolved questions
You weren't just another lover;
You were my best friend.

Winning On It's Own
02/18/17

Some battles aren't worth fighting for.
What's done is done.
Some battles we take on
Consist of
Wasted Effort. Wasted time.
Dust yourself off and keep going forward.

Healing Slowing Down
04/04/18

Considering that I once loved you,
It hurts me,
To hate you.

Forward
02/27/17

Shattered the smiles I provide
Disengaged; unfolding the seed of singleness
Our wings are moving rapidly
Animosity building
Pressure forced outward
It's the end of commitment
Breakup accomplished

Realizations
02/27/17

Fuck your disinterest with my high standards, I deserve it.
You say I want too much but really I am too much for you to
take in whole.

Open Wide
07/18/17

The love we limit,
Limits our happiness.

No Coincidence
03/27/18

sometimes
what we fear
we become

love, you say
you're not like the others
yet it's exactly
what you represent

at times
we create
what we
defend against.

Cleansing
02/27/17

Solitude can be relieving and almost cleansing
Sometimes it stings in your being when you have the sensa-
tions of missing someone
Being alone hearing your own silence is troubling but posi-
tively compromising for the soul

A Work in Progress
03/28/18

so often
I find myself
so wrong
intuition diluted
lust disrupts
the love
I want

Pain from the Heart
02/27/17

Allow me to bear with this heart ache at my own pace. If I
have to break down and lose myself in this battle, it will all be
worth it. World, be patient with me.

Glowing Love
03/01/17

Kissing until we see the moon peak
We're stars trapped above surface
Wrapped around darkness;
We're glowing
There's hope when the blind sense this sight
Sparkles shimmering through the night
Is this a result of our glistening love?
Our chemistry causing chemical reactions
We are Luminescence

A Deeper Cut
01/17/18

Thick Skin
but you still manage to scratch me

Value
03/07/17

Notes to self:
If they take, take ,take
Leave before it's too late,
Because you aren't like them.
You are open.
Don't let them,
Pull valuable components of you.

Building
03/07/17

Fighting like crazy
Because I'm conscious
Of deserving something worthy in my life
Building structure for the bigger picture
Working for my last name vs the first
It's the imprints I leave that mean everything.
Legacy is the objective
I'm moving mountains with my mind.
My future is a result of the hard work of
Me Myself and I.

Unfulfilled Adult Lives
03/15/17

Underneath the surface
Behind business clothes and coffee breathe in the early
mornings
There is a pinch of aching passion
Seething; heavy breathing and regret digested into his lips
As he speaks the anger lingers right off of his skin
Like poison breathe to a kid
A nightmare in the flesh

Why live to survive?

To Love in Vain
03/23/17

I was frozen in the present
Loving a human so selfish
Always claiming that I wanted too much
Willing to still love me,
only if he loves me less
To minimize my standards

All he really wanted was to
See me smaller
But it should have been me
That stopped this mess before catastrophe happened
I didn't love myself enough at the time though
Now I do

Congruency
03/28/17

What I accept in my life won't always be in congruent with what I am capable of receiving.

Helplessness

And I'm tired of running around in circles
Carrying my heart on my sleeve
And it doesn't seem to learn
That my patience is drained
Love stains in my veins,
Yet pain knows me better
Calls me by the name
And fines joy in it

transcendence of love
04/02/17

All that I'm becoming
Is all that I am
All that is transforming
Is all that was corrupt
All of you that still remains
Is everything I'm not

How is it
That your darkness
Becomes magnified in me?
How is it
That I'm shining
But suffocating?
I'm growing and I'm breaking?
I'm revolting but I'm appreciating?
-I'm rising above

Swinging Doors
04/04/17

You touch me with words
I can feel your innocence on my skin
You speak to me with feelings
I reply with full on vulnerability
I feel naked in my own skin
Because you see beyond it,
Straight through it,
I'm an open door
Swinging
So that someone like you
Can enter and close it.

Lisa Marie
102616

As she progresses, the pain manifests
But her beauty transcends
The love she now carries is revitalizing
Enticing
She is not searching for something to feel complete
She is royalty and
She is taking back what is all hers
Queenin' in her Queendom
She used to hide in the dark surfaces of her heart
Now everything in her is enough
She became resourceful, equipped
Any challenge challenging her
She oozes confidence.
Leaving her enemies in delusion
Her pain caused her balance,
Elegance
Out of her internal hell,
She gave birth to a new strength
She has blossomed by pressure, by pain, by hate
By all the energies that cultivate
VIOLENCE
And so it brought her silence
Hushing the pain
Voicing the sounds of her heart
Within her she cried out
Change
She finally received the message
She finally broke the bondage
She's internally free
from me

Infectious Presence
11/17/16

Your luminous state
Releases personal power into each being
You're planting the seeds of greatness in our minds
Meanwhile encouraging us and by being giving
Whoever walks your way and discovers your strengths,
Becomes infectious with your presence.
Don't change.

My "Tough" Men
11/25/16

Listen
I insist
You keep your coat on
You wear a wig
Hoping no one would notice
What's underneath your brown skin
Your fake emotions
You keep your coat on
Carrying the burden
Of it all

You see
All that luggage-
Defense mechanisms

You publicize your strengths
Like your money and your fame
But what you crave,
Is the profundity of it all

You are built with
The mission to being king
But what will serve you as king,
Are not materialistic things
Or surface level feelings
You're trapped
You've built tall, strong walls around you-
Your own Atlantis.
And you feel yourself sinking

It seems like your pleasure has been
What hurts you

If only I could break your walls
When your eyes are shut
So you could see what you have closed off
Without fully seeing and
Best believe,
You will be just fine here too.

Limitless Living
12/04/16

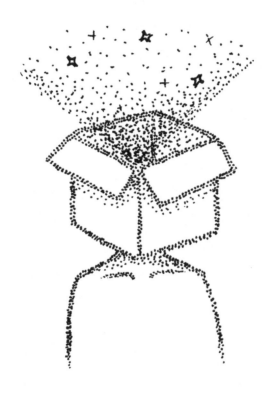

Most live inside their boxes
Drive in them, think in them and are deeply wounded with
this spirit
They even sleep in it
Eat out of a box, speak to a box, watch TV from a box
Where is the road to exit the imprisonment?
Of limiting living?
limiting thinking?
Break free
From the chains of your prison
And this Boxed life we live in

Do things different
Dance to the beat, sing to the rhythm
Feel your spirit
Entirely
And remember,
There are more shapes
Than what we have been conditioned
To believe

Not Skin Deep
05/15/17

I don't want that short term high
I don't need a spliff to my lips
To temporarily relieve me from loneliness.
I want to feel realness, purity, deep conversations.
I don't want to touch a soul with my body,
I want to touch and feel things without any sensations.

Nothing in Common
03/28/18

I search for mountains
you look for the hills
And you prefer the lakes
I bathe in oceans
allowing it all to consume me
I dive deep in it
You just watch

Ideal Partner
07/16/17

Sweet
Selfless
&
Sexual
But
With
Self control

Unconditional
02/24/17

I'm a love worth knowing

A love that stays
has no comprehension
of your flaws
no limitations

Absolute and full

To only love you
would be too simple

I would speak
your language of love
and
forever
adore you

Karma
02/26/17

Leave it to her; do not seek it on your own

She will mirror your pain and let it transfer

She is someone the good people love,

the angry ones hate

She is your best friend,

Her name is Karma.

Ingrained Misogyny
02/09/17

There are those who you are like who understand
The misogyny, entrenched prejudices, preconceived notions
Towards our own women

Then, there are those who are closed
Small minds who kill souls with their words
With language that dispose nonsense

And we wonder why their tongues cut us like swords
And our women have gone mad
And the disturbances are so common. Voices seem silenced.

We have more on the edge of confusion
We have bystanders slowly digesting their conclusions
We have wars with three types of humans

It's time we raise consciousness to society
It's time we construct and rewrite modern day female
philosophy.
It's time we ignite the desire to enlight.

Forever Lips
02/09/17

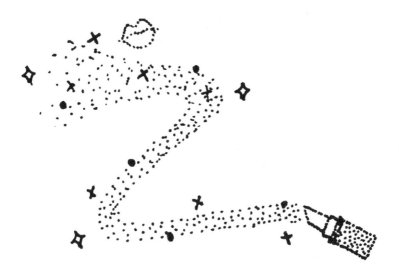

What is more as real, as memorable, as elusive
Than a soft kiss from a lovers lips
Rooted with endless love to give.

Thoughts
12/07/16

Take me back to the time when loving you was easy.
And when you made it seem like loving me wasn't so hard.

An Uneasy Mirror
12/10/16

Suddenly,
he hissed
his language teared down my confidence
he scorned at me
told me I was useless.
told me I need more drive
a stronger why in life
and found me less attractive

And so I became a wild forest fire
and a hurricane
fought with my feelings
so I could receive the lessons

I died
and
brought me back to life
I transcended
into another me
forming, gathering, rebuilding
everything he didn't see

He should have realized

she's just a reflection of me

Painful Growth
12/10/16

I hate you,
for puncturing the vessel of love that was attached to my
heart.
It only drips now,
small droplets of kindness brushing through this empty heart
you had.
The drought,
or shall I say the insufficiency or even better yet,
the dehydration in my heart fills me with too much of
nothing.
I've been deserted in an empty ocean
waiting slowly so that my single droplets shift to rivers of love.
I hate you and I thank you,
for augmenting my vibration.

The Wind and its' Waves
04/21/18

Powerful enough to drown you
soft enough to caress you

I am the earth's feelings manifested into reality

soothing to your soul
I can be your peace

If you could just
see me, breathe me, feel me
while I am at ease
I am a wild vibration with a mind of its own

I'm so many things,
Time studies me,
And is still listening

a hurricane, a cyclone
tsunami, tornado

gentle breeze, the clarity you need
I do it all,
from the rise and the fall,
And yet,
I look at you and think,
we're all too similar

Smiles
12/24/16

My soul smiles when I gaze into your eyes
Your stares they cut me deep like kitchen knives
You're looking at me
Surprised
There's a silent shift
You can't hear it, but the atmosphere says it all.
My senses know but my mind can't seem to control
The fantasy of lasting
The secrets that whisper through this wind
They're advising me
I have admired, grown and adored you
But now it seems like this is the end
And the beginning
Of hearing my heart crackling
While yours breaks free
No one's noticing
My smiles are pretending

takers disguised as lovers
12/25/16

you played your script
excellently
you know how to pretend
there's an applause in the audience
even a standing ovation.
I didn't get the memo
that it was all an act

Congrats you are rewarded and entitled,
so I'll give you my heart,
I'll capture my soul
And send it to multiple years of your
adventurous destinations
since your self obsession does you so good
you will be just fine and I
I will be alright.
you belong to your selfish dedications
may this token of love
gift you in your
pursuit of you.

Broken Love
02/28/17

This never went well with me;
to be tolerated more than I was appreciated.

Velvet Red Lips
12/07/16

Innocence on your lips
The sweet color of sun kissed
Are expressions of you

Bitterness
In the tightness of your grips
Perhaps it's from the passionate
Relationships
That is no longer seeking your attention
Or is it?
Let this endless love come to fruition

There's a slight limp in your steps
A couple bruises on your legs
Your body
So damn sensitive
There's velvet red
Lipstick on your neck
Rough edges on your hips
My fingertips caressing your skin
Flat surface on your stomach
Sharpness on the sides of your fists
Madness when you drift,
Focus

This love is deeper than the ocean
Alas- you're unnoticed
There's been a fire lit inside you
What more of you, needs to be fed?
Fear has spread all over your aching legs
You're frozen

Is the feeling of me
Too intense?

Be Careful
03/28/18

You don't always mirror those who you are like
Did you know
Mosquitoes are also attracted to the light?
Attractive people
Have a way of attracting all types of things.

Deeper Waters
12/27/16

You can almost hear the palm trees melody
The breeze is so soft its warming me up
Deeper waters arrive
The angels are in disbelief
There's nothing just as vivid as this
No unprecedented plot twists
An outline of an image known
Yet there are more pieces to this puzzle
As I explore this grand manor
An island anointed with joy
I conclude this is home.

A Sinking Ocean
12/29/16

Contemplating,
I really, really like this.
But should I allow myself to be swept by love
And focus on it?
Thrilling compulsions but I'm fighting this
War zone between my mind and what's in between my legs
I'm falling fast without direction
With you, I lose my atlas
My thoughts keep drowning when you lightly touch me
I love it.
I'm in tuned with you but am I ready for this?
Will you fill up the holes around my chest?
I'm a mess.
I have forgotten the road to my entrance
Will you help me find it
Because…

I keep sinking in your ocean.

Old Lovers Collide
03/20/17

My lips tasted you once again
All I felt was confusion
I know this isn't right but it's all too familiar
It feels like home
But the dirty, perfume scented,
Light grey shirt that lies on your bed sheets
Reminds me
You're not where I reside in anymore.
That shirt does not belong to me,
And neither do you.

Jealousy
03/20/17

i'm on a mission
to Become
better than I was yesterday
to live a purpose fulfilled life
they cheer me on
but they rather see me below them.
fake gifts
pretend comments
imitation friends
breaks my heart
to see how low
they are willing to go.
it's all a result of insecurity though.
love them anyways
lead with Love

True Strength
03/01/17

She was tough.
Never keeping her emotions
Bottled up.

LISA OSORIO

Boundaries
03/38/18

DO NOT
touch my body
before knowing my heart

Better Off Alone
04/19/18

I crave depth

You crave women
Skin and bones
I look in souls
And think patience
You beg for it
Instant gratification

And I wonder why
I give them chances
And just like the lottery
It is rare,
To find a win

My Confessions
03/07/17

My heart sinks in,
Full with emotions
Feeling of numbness
Craving you deeper
In my dreams
Without even thinking
You have conquered my subconscious
I'm falling into your quicksand
Without hesitations of going nowhere
You have unplugged my resistance
To love without limits
xo
These are my confessions

You Don't Belong To Me
04/20/17

Tell me
Is it value that I bring?
it seems like I'm another errand
that you need to take care of
on your to do list.
I know I'm foolish
I let you spin me like a bottle
until my mind goes weary
so that my eyes could go numb
to everything we did not become.
And yet my lips
Lick your skin
As if they belong to you
But come on
haven't we had enough?
My love has shut off
I no longer want to be wrapped up
in your daring arms singing, "We Belong Together."
Separation is what I'm after
because we don't make love anymore
we make disasters.
We drag each other down like anchors.
I'm shattered up glass
and I'm not partaking
in the destruction of me
No longer
You don't belong to me.

Safe Men
02/27/17

I get it.
You want the man who is soft. Easy to touch.
You want them because their walls are built up.
Do not enter signs are everywhere.
No access to unraveling you.
They wear cover ups like blankets, and masks
You want the man who is afraid to date
but embraces the beauty of skin and romance
if it is effective.
You want the man who is empty like glass,
will crush your words,
and break you before you allow yourself to feel for them.
You are familiar with these men. You chase them.
You attracted this.

You created lust to defend your heart from love.

Bitter Truths
10/28/17

I am not changing who I am
For what you want me to be
I am not your Barbie

Coming To My Senses
04/12/18

If my ears were mute
But I'd have eyes to see

Maybe, just maybe
I'd pay more attention
On what they do not
Pretend to do

I would become a
Believer of their truth
Instead of their lies

Selfish Needs
1/08/17

I love too much.

I also give.
And give.
Too much.

Would you give more?

Would you love me more?

Or would you want
To see me on my knees
Giving you everything

Would you do the same for me?
Because I'm no longer settling.

Casual Bodies
1/08/17

Wait
for me.

If you are casual with my body,
You will be casual with my heart.

I want more.
than casual relations
a love so essential
so grounded I drown in the foundation
roots so strong nothing can break the bond
an attraction to the heart
beyond the infatuation society has inspired upon us
beyond lust. beyond the mediocre.

Falling Feathers
03/23/17

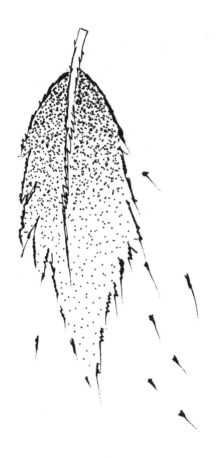

I feel it coming;
Winds heavy sensation trickling through the hairs above my
skin.
Reminders of desires to do more than just survive
Is pushing me to corners to self-evaluate my belonging
My place, my aura, my soul drags
Me to the waters to discuss privately
The trees, the breeze, the sand, the mists, the wind

Feeling so in sync
What distinguishes us from them?
What guides us in the clouds?
Are us humans so similar to trees?
Do we mimic them?
The earth's mysteriousness
Scatters like Doves
And it reminds me that we evolve
Like butterflies.
We're never really gone.
Our purest form is beyond physical
Belief is just the excuse to choose perception
The truth lies not in facts but in intuition
Tasting truth on a lovers lips
Heavy feathers falling from unintended occurrences
The strange synchronicities like reading poetry
To find the fuel to set ablaze the power coming unto you

Detachment
04/11/17

These circles need endings
We can't keep kissing each other
Like longtime lovers
Every time we break up.
We need an end.
Clarity release us out of this fog,
Out of this matrix,
Out of this game that has no winning.
We mix up lessons with soulmates and devotions,
See our love stumbles upon us
But we are broken.

The Shallow One
03/27/18

We're not the same
you say you want me
but darling
that. is. not. enough.
the picture painted
is weak
my heart is too big
to love multiple men in pieces
you see my pretty flower
cut me from my source
put me in your vase
and as you see my beauty in your room
with time you watch me die

the water you feed me is nice,
But I need more sunlight

see darling
the way I'd treasure you
I'd keep you where you shall bloom
and take you to places
disregarding my selfish desires
take notes
so the good things that come into your life
Don't always search for the exit signs.

Mount Everest
1/01/17

A selection of hills and mountains
She chose the mountain
Intentionally crossing the yellow caution signs
Because that road was unexplored.
Cracked bones,
Scratches from the floor
But skin deep pain did not hit home
Gasping for air
An altitude so high
Yet she could not quit
Her own will conquered her, controlling her
She looked forward for the echoes of the wind,
The silent song she itched for
She was in love with the secrets planted in
The mysteries of the world
Even if it physically destroyed her

A therapeutic pleasure
A spirit deep need
She's obsessed
She lets go of nonsense
Thoughts
When she hikes the unknown treasures
Of Mount Everest.

Greedy Shits
1/03/17

How dare you pick up all the fruits and not share any with
me
When I got the seeds and I watered them daily
I built the roots but you got greedy
How dare me not teach myself how to bloom
Because look at what I did to you.

Small Stones
1/03/17

When it's too late,
You will see me shine
From the insides to my outsides

You will realize I was that diamond all along
And you were too busy for me
Collecting small stones.

Me Without You
04/14/17

My soul splits into two
As if it's supposed to
One with me and one with you
And soul suffers
And soul mourns the loss
And soul wants the rest of her back
But she's hesitant
She's troubled
Because we bend
We break, we make mistakes
Our hearts can't take
We ache
We separate
We fly across galaxies
And fall down to sea level
It's authentic, but it's tragic
Like storms in an island
Car crashes
After they've already happened
A dive with a bad landing
It's a beautiful disaster
So my soul remains in two
It's better off apart

To prevent extremities of feelings
That should no longer be of concern

03/28/18

DO NOT
ENTERtain
unsustainable
Love

Gentle Openings
02/11/18

I'm all yours until further notice
I'm all in, and this is dangerous
not trying to put my feelings
on my sleeves
but there they are taunting me
you read me completely, discreetly
you know me,
You have broken down my walls
and my limits as to what I should do with you
have disappeared
Taking a chance,
I welcome you in

Lady Like Me
2008

Sad to my soul
So unhappy as can be
Still keeping my head up
Because that is how
A lady like me
Ought to be
Slowly rising up
Recovering bad luck
Doing what is right
Saying goodbye to the wrong
Denying what we had
Like in a love song
Regretting saying yes
Wish I told you no
So long in the past,
I should have let you go

Vulnerable
05/17/17

I write my heart out
And let you see

A Happy Funeral
04/25/17

I buried my jealousy
Held the ceremony
Threw my hand picked purple roses
Above its grave
May it rest in peace
And now I celebrate this
For I am cleansing.
I do not bleed out insecurity
It doesn't sting when I'm fighting
Moral consciousness
I am present, I am free
These hands don't write out of resentment
It's all love.

My Lotus
04/25/17

I am not your average flower
That you can grow and harvest and pluck and pull
I'm one that lives outside of your control; I'm on my own
I manifest my development; I bloom.
Not from the weather but by what I bring to reap
Unapologetic, I embrace me.
I refuse to remove the stubborn thorns that may sting you,
And make me, me
I am no broken spirit, I am divine
Being less of me to impress you
Is a fabrication to my character; a false impression.
I am the flower that you will see grow so tall
Emotionally, intellectually, spiritually
Through the dimensions of my awakenings
That you will be drawn to me like bees to honey.
My moist stems, my prickly thorns,
My non perfect, velvety petals are far from insecurity.
The fault in my flaws is a mental judgment

That's dismissive because my soil is my incubator for growth
and love.
I feed it kindness.
I feed it adoration,
Positive affirmations,
Powerful incantations.
I gather this vibrancy that consists of my liveliness, and my
exuberance,
And transfer it.
I mirror my mind
My foundation is simply exotic;
Built on mixtures of mud, dirt and water
I grow from it
Rebirth from it
Compelling. Captivating.
My Lotus

Fears
05/22/17

The moment I grab a piece to your map
That in hopes it will guide me
I read the title and see that I have a thousand pieces to unravel
I want to stay, I want to appreciate,
I want to love you with my entire being
But I'm afraid
I'll never be able to find all the pieces to this maze
and you'll hide and find a better navigator.

07/05/17

I would love you so much
On purpose
So you could love yourself
On accident

The Last Chapter
05/10/18

If I can do it
So can you

The wind and its' waves
Are here for you

May you read and reread this book
And remind yourself
You have gone through it all
And look at how beautifully
You are becoming.

Lead with love.

I appreciate you all.
Thank you.

Made in the USA
Coppell, TX
23 May 2021

56197232R10066